The Alchemy Of Existence

Cheyenne DeMara

India | USA | UK

Copyright © Cheyenne DeMara
All Rights Reserved.

This book has been self-published with all reasonable efforts taken to make the material error-free by the author. No part of this book shall be used, reproduced in any manner whatsoever without written permission from the author, except in the case of brief quotations embodied in critical articles and reviews.

The Author of this book is solely responsible and liable for its content including but not limited to the views, representations, descriptions, statements, information, opinions, and references ["Content"]. The Content of this book shall not constitute or be construed or deemed to reflect the opinion or expression of the Publisher or Editor. Neither the Publisher nor Editor endorse or approve the Content of this book or guarantee the reliability, accuracy, or completeness of the Content published herein and do not make any representations or warranties of any kind, express or implied, including but not limited to the implied warranties of merchantability, fitness for a particular purpose.

The Publisher and Editor shall not be liable whatsoever...

Made with ❤ on the BookLeaf Publishing Platform
www.bookleafpub.in
www.bookleafpub.com

Dedication

To the ones that matter to me the most and have contributed to the alchemy of my own personal experiences. You've had your hands, and often your hearts, in the shaping of who I am today. Family, friends, lovers - I'm sure you'll read and know exactly the page you've inspired. Love always.

To the ones who think they don't matter at all- you too, have a page and have made an impact greater than you can imagine.

To the ones who hurt me- you know what they say...if the shoe fits.

To my soul that exists outside of my body, Atlas, the only I shall dedicate to by name- I hope that I always make you at least as half as proud as I am of you. Mommy loves you always.

And ultimately to those who carry spirit and burden of the human heart, may you ever persist.

Preface

These are mere inner ramblings. Take what resonates, leave what doesn't. This is just a small piece of the greater whole that makes up the (my) early adulthood experience.

What a blessing to have loved, longed, lost and then some.

Acknowledgements

Thank you to all of the people who have contributed to this amazing thing called life. Thank you, God, for blessing me with all the intricacies that have led to me being where I am at today. And special thanks to me- for committing myself to a project I never thought I'd get done- all while momming, schooling, and working like the busy madwoman I have always strived to be.

Love Language

I am desperate to learn your language
But not a syllable slips from my lips.

Love, a foreign dialect, an ancient art.
A careful craft created in bated breath.

How have such articulated verses been born
In the rafters of a radical reaction
To love requited?

Only a literary scholar could describe the way
Apprehensive, anxious longing
Transposes itself into the love of a lifetime.

Linguistic tactics are not enough to decipher
The happenings of the heart.

But let me begin practicing my knowledge
Of the universal language of the body.

My lips will linger a little longer,
I will feel your body as it melts into mine.
Speaking in silence,
My favorite love language.

Pancakes

There are so many ways to eat pancakes.
Some people use syrup and butter.
Others like it plain or with fruit.
Do you dip yours one piece at a time?
Or do you let it ooze down a tall stack?
Do you take yours with a side of coffee?
Or would you prefer a glass of orange juice?

Would you rather have French toast?
For me- sweet is not the way to go.

I'll take a coffee, strong and hearty.
An English muffin and homemade jam.

Then again,
There's also the simplicity of cereal.
Or so you would think.
There's so many to choose from.
Are you choosing the childish, colorful loops?
Do you like the old-man bran?

Or do you fall somewhere in the middle-
Maybe a slightly sweet wheat.

So many little things to learn about each other,
And it could all start over the first meal of the day.

All I can hope is that regardless of how you like your
pancakes served,
You prefer to have them next to me.

Timeless

The monotony of motherhood
leaves nothing to the imagination.
From sun up to sun down,
Using the clock as validation.

5 more minutes, you say
As the alarm goes off.
15 more minutes go by,
You never get to sleep enough.

1 more hour to go,
Then the kids go to school.
Getting everyone ready,
Sticking to the schedule.

Everyone is away on their day,
You clean and run errands.
4 more hours is plenty,
Maybe you can take a break from being a parent.

30 minutes in line for a coffee,
Expensive and sweet.
It's not worth the money,
Even though it's a nice treat.

More time to spare,
But it is time to come home.
Dinner needs prepping,
There is no time to roam.

The traffic is bad,
it is just my luck
5 minutes laying on the horn.
Is it already time for pick-up?

The kids are back,
It's time to do homework.
Then dinner is eaten,
The dishes stacked perked.

30 minutes more to draw up a bath,
Then it is the bedtime routine
"Please lay down"
No one wants to deal with a mother's wrath.

Snuggled up in bed as time starts to slow
Soft, little lashes flutter

A small hand that won't let go.

Tiny breaths up against your cheek,
You pull your head up from the pillow
And take a quick peek.

Peacefully asleep, now it is time to slip away.
But sometimes in this moment, you just want to stay.

The day was crazy, just like any other.
Never enough time, the children grow up.
Clocks tick on, but who does it bother?

8 more hours until the day starts anew,
An ache in the heart counting the sleep you'll get.
The dishes remain in the sink, what else is there to do?

A deep breathe in,
suds still entangled in your baby's hair.
At least they are clean, I'd call that a win.

It's been at least an hour,
No one has made a sound.
The peace children bring,
It brings a mother true power.

You soak up the minutes,

As all mothers know.
These times are fleeting,
So you don't let go.

How many more minutes?
Your back is to the clock.
Loving your baby, there are no limits.

For the moments when you want more time,
Time Less.

Magic Within

To be made of wonder, awe, fascination,
Powerful forces of nature, righteous beauty.
Spiritual mystery, a magic visionary.

Devoutly tied to existential feelings of
Divinity, unity, and peace.

And yet, esoteric. An arcane knowledge that few appreciate.

The world could use more mystical forces.

And maybe that magic resides within you.

Jack of All Trades

Prowess in theory, master of none.
Looks good on paper,
Yet nothing gets done.

Keeping hands busy,
A façade of success.
No stride in advancement,
The result just more stress.

The time now wasted, you can't get back.
Potential is out there,
It is not something you lack.
Hold steady, don't look at the clock.
Time is a construct,
There is more to unlock.

Greater forces exist; there is more to life.
Confines of accomplishment,
One of life's great strifes.

Prowess in theory, master of one.
Finding love for one another.
There is more to be done.

Curated Love

There is no art truer than that of two lovers.
Two bodies, statuesque, carved marble, entangled in a moment in time.
Passion captured, hearts bleeding desire.

Will you be my Renaissance man?
Allow my hands to sculpt magic that even the Mona Lisa would gawk at?
Da Vinci uncoded, I'm unlocking your body's mysteries.

What would Michelangelo say if he saw
How beautifully the gradient of the marble accentuated your cock?
He might be painting the Creation of Adam,
but I bear witness to the creation of Man.

Then there is Venus, a woman of true beauty.
But did she swallow her man and lick every last drop?
Let me worship your body like a chapel, Sistine.
Let me dine upon your body, ravenous, like my Last

Supper.

What a revival in culture, although the art remains the same.
Explicit male dominance, erotics of absolutism,
The beauty is timeless, just like a good fuck.

Died

Died
Failure to thrive.
I wanted to die.
Consumed by sadness.
I am just trying to survive.

I couldn't save my unborn.
My spirit has been broken,
Never to be pure again.
        My heart has never been so
torn.

How could I pick up the pieces?
My empty womb a constant reminder
Of the one my body betrayed.
A heartbeat ceases.

Not just theirs but mine.
In unison, I believe we both died.
Except I was resurrected,

Barren, alone, looking for a lifeline.

In the waiting room of a hospital.
Bleeding and crying on the floor.
Waiting to be called back before I died.
I was hoping that outcome was possible.

Reborn

Surviving and thriving.
A second chance at life.
Overwhelmed by joy.
A new soul arriving.

Held for so long,
Safe in my belly.
A little boy yet to be born.
My little boy- so very strong.
How could I still have the anxiety?
His little feet kicking,
Arms stretching out wide.
Proof of life inside of me.

A fire reignited.
A bond that was already well fortified
I was redeemed as a woman.
A future that was no longer far-sighted.

In the hospital bed.

Tucked in cozy with my bundle of joy.
Waiting to go home.
The journey of motherhood is ahead.

Polar Bear

Consider me a polar bear.
Seemingly fluffy, warm, and strong.
Most cartoons paint an image, large eyes filled with care.
An animal that would do no wrong.

But If you know your nature facts,
You might be aware that polar bears have 42 teeth.
Ripping apart flesh, it's the only way it knows how to act.
There is a darkness that lies underneath.

Wandering aimlessly, across an artic tundra,
Until it sees a threat or its next meal.
Oh look, a baby seal.

Nothing gets in it's way
From tame to wild
A routine, day to day.
Only being gentle, to soothe it's child.

What a curious thing,
Maybe that is why they call me bi polar.
Bear with me,
I too, have been tranquilized.

Longing

No poem could begin to convey the longing that I have.

The longing for the life I've always imagined, the castles I've built- home to the love I've got burning in my soul.

And the longing for you to live there.

The Table

What do you bring to the table?

Financial security?
Problem-solving skills?
Emotional support?
Valuable communication and honesty?

Some of you sit at the head of the seating arrangement
Awaiting dinner service from the person who quite
literally
Brings it to table.

Who are you to sit there?
You are no man of the house.
This is not the Last Supper.
And you are not my God.

Some of you can't even set the table,
let alone bring anything else to it.
All there is to show for your presence-

A dirty dish display of gluttony

Feasting on what I have to offer
And nothing in return.

Me?

I don't sit at the head of the table.
And I do more than just bringing it to the table.

I am the damn table.

Foundational, strong.
A crucial supporter, essential for function.

And you no longer have a seat.

To Meet You

I didn't have the chance to hold you.
I carried you, but that wasn't enough.

A flicker on a screen captured in black and white.
A moment frozen before things got tough.

Twelve weeks, you had a name.
I hold that close, our little secret.

I'll call for you when I get to Heaven
and when I hear your sweet response
I will know exactly who you are.

I won't even have to look to know it is your soul.
My baby.

I can't wait to meet you.

-Mommy

Dear God

Dear God,

Please let there be a heaven for all creatures.

The roadkill, the trapped mouse.
The spider curled up in my windowsill.

Let them be warm, full, and unafraid.

I know you, God.
And I know that you know me.

Welcome me with the creatures,
as we both have had to bear witness to the cruelty of man.

Let them come to me
So that I may show them the gentle touch of woman
And the gentleness of death.

I shall name them, as one does when the creature comes Home.

Cruise Control

The road is winding
And I'm not good at driving
Someone take the wheel.

The road is winding
What is around the next bend?
A deer in headlights?

The road is winding
My highbeams went out- it's dark
I'm scared of the dark

The road is winding
I am going way too fast.
Where are the damn brakes?

The road is winding
And my car plateaus in air
Off the embankment

The road was winding
And yet I landed unscathed
In my dad's driveway.

The road was winding
My cruise was set to safety
And it led me home.

Blessed

I look at the epitome of beautiful creation that you are daily. You've looked back at me and I feel that I am your world. As your world grows and you grow with it you start to swell with curiousity in which every question must have an answer. When you now say with a boyish grin, "Why are you looking at me?" I say, "Because I love you so much" and what I mean is:

"I hope God doesn't change his mind in lending you to me".

Justice Just Us

Lacking be the justice,
In a country full of malice.
It's not the world versus woman,
Nor is it I versus man.
But there is a war that rages between us.

Equity not possible
With a man who is uncrossable,
Covered ears and blind eyes
As part of a woman's soul dies.
And who is responsible?

We are not seeking the power
Nor have the desire to tower
Over the male populace
But to create a divine, feminine acropolis,
With bodily autonomy, It's ours.

Our values have been deeply buried,
The heavy weight females have carried,

We have been given the right to free speech,
So listen to us scream, cry, and preach.
This common experience of girlhood is not varied.

We have the right to speak
But have not been heard.
Seen as meek, fragile as a bird.
We are strong, don't be mistaken.
Our rally is one to partake in.
This call to action will not be deferred.

So be gone days of unfounded wage gaps,
Cat calls and disrespect only seen as a mishap.
Let's place the value of a woman in heart,
Not in body, a definition of the male patriarch
There is rage within us, we are ready to snap.

Our body is not to be owned.
We are not an object, a uterus to be loaned.
You say the body is a temple,
Yet you continue to heckle.
Our cries made a mockery,
It is no longer an action to be condoned.

We call for justice.
Do not dismiss.
We are tired of fighting

Our souls need relighting
Do it for justice.
Do it for Just Us.

Us being the mothers and daughters,
The wives and the sisters.
Look to your left, now look to your right.
Chances are, you are one among us.

The Children Are Awake

The late-night hum of the tv no longer sounds like George Lopez reruns at 1am. Instead, it is influencer after influencer promoting the latest and greatest from high end face care to low-cost screen-printed tees or worse yet comedy specials turned political jabs, a hoarse laugh the reminder of the human responsibility to grin and bear it.

Going outside to play isn't the same as we can't guarantee that our children will return home safely in the daylight, let alone when the streetlights go on. We have turned in the bug catchers and bubbles for screen time and slime and dear God, I am so grateful for the slime I have to pick out of the carpet because at least I know there was the presence of joy and creativity. But why, why is the slime the same color as the foods offered to the kids and why are they both made of the same compounds and why does only one carry a warning label?

I am a child of yesterday, the adult of today, raising an adult of tomorrow. We awake to the new hums, the new realities of play, and we are adapting and we are changing. It is 1am and the children are awake.

The revolution is awake.

Ramblings of Corporate America

Sale!
Buy one, get one free.
Free gift with purchase.
Apply for the card for the discount!

Discount!
Special, today only!
Check-out by midnight.
Online only deal.

Deal!
Make a deal today!
Bargain with the Devil.
Get it while it's hot!

Hot!
Fire steals on this holiday weekend!
Don't miss out!
Flexible payment plan!

Plan!
Have you planned for retirement?
Have you bought your plot?
Have you bought your ticket into the pearly gates?

Gates.
Bill Gates, Microsoft
Stock Market, Stock Crash
What payment does He accept?

Accept.
Except.
Chip reader not read.
Payment Declined.

Buy now!
Bye now.

XOXO

I hope you hate this poem.
I didn't write it for you.
As per your normal,
You've ignored your cue.

Get up and get out.
Please just go away.
You sit there and cry,
Hoping I'll beg you to stay.

These words are my strength.
I know you see it too.
But deep down I'm broken,
And all along you've enjoyed the view.

No longer will I shed a tear.
For you've collected them in buckets.
You parade about a trophy for your abuse,
This poem is my "fuck it"

Fuck you.

Oh, did I just lose my rhyme scheme?
That doesn't matter to me.
This poem is just requited love,
It is what you deserve it to be.

Do you fear this retribution?
Well, it's time to pay the price.
The cost I know you can't afford.
This is our marriage dissolution.

I hope you like this poem.
Actually, it was for you.
Consider it my parting gift,
From the heart and long overdue.

Hotel

Here I am, just passing through town.
Brought you along for the ride, not expecting much.

We lie in bed,
Fresh sheets.
Awaken to a continental breakfast.

Leaving, things feel different.

I know this was just a hotel stay.
But I hope to have a late check out.

Fin

Fin. Final. End.
Complete. Whole. Done.

Or so you thought.
But so many thoughts are left unwritten.
This is but the beginning of the alchemy in which my life has been spun.

TBC.

www.ingramcontent.com/pod-product-compliance
Lightning Source LLC
Chambersburg PA
CBHW070040070426
42449CB00012BA/3118